I0560362

Give Your Yes a Bestie
Named NO

Testimonials

The BRAVE method will truly help people pleasers like me break that barrier and value their happiness. I loved the questions included at the end of each chapter to break down the process meaningfully. This book will be an excellent resource to help people understand that their boundaries are important for their own personal well-being. This has truly inspired me to challenge myself to set better boundaries for my well-being.

—Amber Harsh

This is a very valuable book. I thought I knew what boundaries were, but Jennifer opened a new door to inner boundaries. This is a must-read for all the people pleasers.

—Peter Simmons

I enjoyed reading this book. Jen illustrated setting boundaries with simple but powerful explanations and followed up with action steps that truly guide you to achieving results. This is a book I will keep handy for when I need assistance with future situations that come up.

–Heather Baker

Reading "Give Your Yes a Bestie Named No" helped me understand the importance of setting boundaries and respecting my personal values guilt-free. Jen's relatable tone and practical examples made it easier for me to say "no" with confidence and clarity. This book felt like a friend cheering me on toward a healthier, more intentional life.

–Michaela Frerichs

I was always a person who would never say no to anyone. With Jen's book, that helped me feel so much better to have boundaries set, and I had more time and didn't feel so pressured.

–Sandra Metzger

'Give Your Yes Needs a Bestie Named No' is a powerful, practical guide for anyone tired of people-pleasing and burnout. Jen Anderson's B.R.A.V.E. method makes boundary-setting feel doable, not daunting. It's honest, empowering, and refreshingly relatable. A must-read for reclaiming your peace.

–Kristen Burrus, Enlighten Services www.kristenburrus.com

Jennifer's book was insightful, and I found the BRAVE concept particularly valuable. It breaks down boundary-setting into actionable steps.

Her perspective that "discomfort is growth in disguise" resonated with me–a powerful reminder that stepping outside our comfort zone leads to meaningful change.

–Karen Dunham

So many examples that are easy to fit your situation into. The review questions in each section help you figure out the best place to begin, and the clear action points make implementation straightforward.

–Kristin Wood

Jen has this great framework for dealing with boundaries. B.R.A.V.E. She broke down her framework so I could better understand and use it. She gave me daily affirmations, action steps, quick tips, challenges, and so much information. This book was an easy read, one that I could go through 6 chapters easily in one hour, and I'm not even a fast reader. I like that it is easy to read and easy to implement. I can start setting up boundaries within my personal relationships, in my job, with technology, and how I can live a boundaried life. I highly recommend this book to anyone who needs help with setting up boundaries!

–Wendy Carlson, Prospering Transactions, LLC; http:// www.prosperingtransactions.com/

This was such an easy read, with so much amazing information. All the examples, action steps, and suggestions were exactly what I needed to help me set better boundaries and release the guilt I used to feel. I feel like I can set boundaries to take care of myself, but still be the compassionate person I want to be. This is a must-read!!!

–Heather Johnson

Give Your YES a Bestie NAMED NO

A PRACTICAL GUIDE
TO SETTING BOUNDARIES WITHOUT
GUILT, FEAR, OR APOLOGY.

JEN ANDERSON

Copyright © 2025 Jen Anderson

All rights reserved. No part of this book may be reproduced or transmitted in any form by any means — electronic, mechanical, photocopying, recording, or otherwise — without prior written permission of the author.

ISBN 979-8-9990819-0-2—Paperback

ISBN 979-8-9990819-1-9 e-Book

Editing by Tara Hayes

Cover design by Biserka Designs

Interior formatting by Kevin Coleman.

Disclaimer

The intended purpose of this book is solely informational and motivational. It is not a substitute for licensed therapy, legal advice, or medical treatment. The author makes no guarantees about the outcome of following the advice contained herein. The author shares all personal stories with permission or has altered them to protect privacy.

Published by Thankful Hearts Coaching

Dedication

To my parents, thank you for instilling in me the values of kindness, hard work, and resilience. I am proud to carry those Midwestern roots into everything I do.

To my husband, thank you for being the steady presence beside me — always encouraging, always believing, and always by my side. Your love and support make everything possible.

To my clients, you are the heartbeat of this work. Every breakthrough, every boundary set, and every brave moment you choose — I grow alongside you. Thank you for trusting me with your transformation and for teaching me as much as I teach you.

To my business besties, Kristin and Tiffani, you remind me what wholehearted support looks like. Thank you for being my sounding board, my hype squad, and my daily reminder that women rise higher when we rise together.

To my mentor and Pastor, Fred Simon,

Thank you for seeing something in me before I could see it in myself. Your wisdom, patience, and unwavering belief guided me through the early steps of this journey. You didn't just teach me about coaching — you taught me how to listen with compassion, lead with integrity, and grow with purpose. Your mentorship laid the foundation for everything I do today, and I carry your guidance with me into every session, every breakthrough, and every life I'm honored to impact.

And to every woman holding space for others while trying to hold it together herself, this is for you.

You are not alone. You are worthy of your own "yes." And you are so, so ready.

Contents

Foreword

As someone who has spent years immersed in the science of mindset, teaching people how to become the boss of their brains and reclaim their lives from burnout and people-pleasing, I can say this with absolute certainty: Jen Anderson gets it.

In Give Your YES a Bestie Named NO, Jen doesn't just offer another self-help blueprint. She delivers a powerful, practical, and deeply compassionate guide for learning how to set boundaries without guilt, shame, or apology. Her B.R.A.V.E. method is exactly what the world needs right now — especially women who have spent far too long saying "yes" to everyone else at the expense of their own well-being.

What struck me most while reading this book was how beautifully Jen blends real-talk with real science — and real soul. She invites us in with honesty and humor, holds space for our struggles, and gently but firmly reminds us that saying "no" isn't rejection; it's redirection toward a life that aligns with our values, our peace, and our truth.

As a mindset speaker, TEDx presenter, and creator of Mindcraft University, I speak frequently about intentional living. I teach about rewiring the brain for positivity, presence, and authenticity. And what Jen teaches in these pages mirrors that mission precisely. Because here's the thing: Boundaries aren't just external guardrails — they are internal declarations of self-worth. Every "no" we speak with confidence is really a "yes" to ourselves.

Whether you're a lifelong people-pleaser, someone recovering from chronic burnout, or just a human being trying to show up as your best and brightest self, this book is your permission slip to reclaim your time, energy, and joy.

So go ahead. Say yes to Jen. Say yes to you.

Because you are so, so worth it.

—Dr. Kimberly Quinn
Founder and CEO of Mindcraft University
TEDx Speaker | Psychology Today Contributor

Introduction

E ver catch yourself automatically saying "yes" when every cell in your body is screaming "please, no!"?

Take a deep breath with me.

Picture this: It's Thursday afternoon, and your calendar looks like a game of Tetris gone wrong. Your colleague needs help with their presentation, the PTA is begging for volunteers, and your best friend wants you to host a dinner party... tomorrow. Your mouth opens, and that familiar, "Sure, I can help!" slips out, while your inner voice is having a complete meltdown.

If you're nodding right now, you're in exactly the right place.

Here's the truth: Saying "no" isn't just about turning things down –it's your permission slip to saying "YES!" to happiness. And I'm not talking about that surface-level, people-pleasing kind of happy. I'm talking about that deep-in-your-soul, finally-breathing-freely, this-is-what-authenticity-feels-like kind of joy.

As Maya Angelou wisely said, "When someone shows you who they are, believe them the first time." The same goes for your inner wisdom when it tells you it's time to set a boundary. That little voice? It's your personal GPS guiding you toward peace.

Let me introduce you to something called the B.R.A.V.E method (because everything's better with a framework, right?). It starts with boundaries–those invisible, yet powerful lines that protect your peace like a force field of self-respect. But unlike a fortress wall, these boundaries aren't about shutting people out; they're about letting your authentic self shine.

When you're crystal clear about your limits, you're not being diffi-cult–you're being deliberate. You're saying, "I value myself enough to protect my time and energy!" And that clarity? It's a gift not just to you, but to everyone around you.

Will everyone immediately understand and respect your newly established boundaries? Probably not. There might still be those persistent requests for "just one more small favor." That's okay, because this book isn't just about setting boundaries; it's about becoming unshakeable in maintaining them.

Think of your boundaries like your favorite comfort food recipe – they need to be just right for you, nourishing enough to sustain you, and strong enough to keep you satisfied.

In this book, we'll explore the transformative B.R.A.V.E method:

B: Boundaries: Setting & maintaining clear limits

R: Recognize & Release: Identifying patterns & letting go of guilt

A: Authentic Action: Taking steps that align with YOUR truth

V: Validate & Value: Because "yes" doesn't measure your worth

E: Empower & Evolve: Growing into your most authentic self)

Daily Affirmation: "I honor my boundaries with confidence and grace. My 'no' is as powerful as my 'yes.'"

Get ready to transform from a people-pleaser to a peace-keeper. We're about to embark on a journey that will help you reclaim your time, your energy, and, most importantly, your joy. And the best part? No more lying awake at night wondering how you'll manage all those commitments you wish you hadn't made.

Remember: Progress over perfection. Your boundary-setting skills might be a work in progress right now, but that's exactly where transformation begins.

Ready to get B.R.A.V.E together?

Let's do this!

PART ONE

The Truth About Boundaries

The truth is, boundaries aren't barriers — they're the bridges that lead you back to yourself.

— JEN ANDERSON

Affirmation:

"I deserve boundaries that honor my truth, protect my peace, and reflect my worth."

1. *The Yes Mess*

HOW WE GOT HERE

"The only people who get upset about you setting boundaries are the ones who benefited from you having none."

— UNKNOWN

You know that feeling when your phone buzzes with yet another request, and your stomach does that little flip? The one where you already know you should say no, but your mouth is getting ready to say yes anyway?

Deep breath - we're about to change that dance forever.

Here's the truth: Boundaries aren't just another self-help buzzword. They're your personal force field protecting your time, energy, and sanity. Think of them as your very own "Terms and Conditions" for life– except people actually need to read these!

What's a Boundary, really? Remember playing "the floor is lava" as a kid? You knew exactly where you could and couldn't step. Boundaries are like that, but for your adult life. They're your personal rulebook for how you want to be treated, what you'll accept, and what makes you say, "Thanks, but that's a hard pass from me!"

LET'S BREAK IT DOWN - THE DIFFERENT FLAVORS OF BOUNDARIES:

1. **Emotional Boundaries** (The Heart Guards): These are your emotional VIP security team. When your coworker starts dumping their daily drama during your lunch break, your emotional boundary might sound like: "I hear that you're going through a lot, but I need to protect my own emotional energy right now."

   Let me share a boundary breakthrough moment from my past (because yes, even your boundary coach had to learn these lessons the hard way!). Picture this: I'm working in an office where apparently everyone thought they had "Boss" stamped on their forehead. You know the type - the ones who treat your office like their personal venting lounge? There was this one colleague (let's call him Mr. Rant-and-Rave) who had turned dropping by my office into an Olympic sport. He'd storm in, already mid-rant, using my space as his personal therapy session, minus the therapy part and a lot of unnecessary drama.

   One day, something in me just ... shifted. Maybe it was the third interruption before coffee, or maybe my inner boundary queen finally decided to wake up, but I had this crystal-clear moment: "I am not anyone's verbal punching bag."

So, channeling my inner calm-but-firm goddess (trust me, she was in there somewhere!), I stood up, stepped between him and my desk, and walked him slowly—yes, slowly—backward toward the door. Picture it: one small step at a time, like the world's most intentional dance.

Then, in my most centered voice (the one I now use with coaching clients), I said, "When you're ready to speak to me like a human being, I would love to help you with whatever is upsetting you. But until then, you're not welcome in my office anymore."

The look on his face? Priceless. I'm pretty sure he was wondering who body-snatched his usual pushover. But here's the magic part - from that day forward, this man KNOCKED ON MY DOOR. "Do you have time to see me? I need to discuss something." Complete transformation.

Why did it work? Because sometimes people need a clear, firm boundary to respect you. Nobody in that office had ever shown him where the line was - until that day.

The lesson? Your boundaries can be both kind and firm. You don't need to scream or throw things (though trust me, I have considered it). You just need to stand in your worth and calmly show others how to treat you.

2. **Material Boundaries** (The Mine-Not-Yours Zone)
   Remember when your sister "borrowed" your favorite sweater and returned it with mysterious stains? Material boundaries are your "what's mine is mine" guidelines. And no, Karen, from accounting, that doesn't mean your desk is the office supply store.

3. **Intellectual Boundaries** (The Mind Matters): These protect your thoughts and beliefs. When someone dismisses your ideas or tries to force their opinions on you, your intellectual boundary might say, "We can disagree and still respect each other."
4. **Physical Boundaries** (The Personal Space Bubble) Your body, your rules. Whether it's the hugger at work or the close-talker at parties, you get to decide your comfort zone. No explanation needed!
5. **Time Boundaries** (The Calendar Keeper) Because your time isn't an all-you-can-eat buffet for others (to feast on). "Sorry, my schedule is full" is a complete sentence!

WHY BOUNDARIES ARE YOUR NEW BEST FRIEND:

They're Your Personal Bodyguard

Protecting your energy isn't selfish—it's necessary.

Like putting on your own oxygen mask first on a plane, boundaries ensure you have enough energy to actually help others--if you choose to.

They're Your Relationship Super-Glue

Plot twist: Good boundaries actually create better relationships!

When people know where they stand, there's less room for resentment and more space for genuine connection.

They're Your Identity Anchor

Without boundaries, you're like a leaf in the wind, going wherever others blow you.

With them, you're the tree—rooted, strong, and clear about who you are.

Daily Affirmation: "My boundaries are acts of self-respect, not walls of self-defense."

REFLECTION CORNER:

Pause here for a moment.

1. Think about a time when you wished you'd set a boundary but didn't. What stopped you?
2. What's one boundary you could set this week that would make the biggest positive impact on your life?
3. Which type of boundary (emotional, material, etc.) do you find hardest to maintain? Why?

Power Moves for Your Boundary-Setting Journey:

- Start small - practice saying, "let me check my calendar," instead of an immediate yes
- Use "I" statements - "I need..." instead of "You should..."
- Remember: Discomfort is growth in disguise

B.R.A.V.E ACTION STEPS:

B - Begin by identifying one boundary you need most right now

R - Recognize what happens when this boundary is crossed

A - Act on setting this boundary in a small way today

V - Validate your right to have this boundary

E - Evolve by practicing this boundary daily

Remember: Progress over perfection. Your boundary-setting muscles might be a little weak right now, but just like any other muscle, they'll get stronger with practice.

Quote to Keep Close:

"Boundaries are the distance at which I can love you and me simultaneously."

— PRENTIS HEMPHILL

---

2. The People-Pleasing Puzzle

WHY SETTING BOUNDARIES FEELS LIKE ROCKET SCIENCE

You can be a good person with a kind heart and still say no.

— UNKNOWN

Remember the last time you checked your phone and saw three different group chats, planning three different events, all happening on the same weekend? And somehow, you're supposed to be at ALL of them?

Deep exhale

Let's talk about why saying "no" feels harder than trying to fold a fitted sheet.

Here's the truth: If setting boundaries were easy, we wouldn't be here having this conversation. But for most of us (especially the recovering people-pleasers in the room), setting boundaries feels about as comfortable as wearing shoes on the wrong feet.

WHY WE'RE STUCK IN THE "YES" CYCLE

The Good Girl/Guy Programming

Remember being told "be nice" or "don't make waves" growing up? Yeah, we've all got that voice in our head saying, "good people don't say no."

Plot twist: The kindest people actually DO say no –they're just better rested than the rest of us!

The Guilt Games

You know that feeling when you finally say no and your stomach does more flips than an Olympic gymnast?

That's not your intuition—that's years of people-pleasing programming setting off false alarms.

The "What If" Worries

- What if they don't like me anymore?
- What if I hurt their feelings?
- What if they never ask me again?

Spoiler alert: Real friends stick around ... even when you have boundaries!

The Clarity Confusion

Sometimes we're so used to putting others first that we don't even know what WE want. It's like trying to follow a GPS that's speaking a language we don't understand.

Let me share a quick story about my client Sarah (name changed for privacy). She was a successful business owner who came to me feeling completely burned out. Every time a client asked for a rush job, she'd say yes. Every time her family needed something, she'd drop everything. She was the go-to person for everyone's emergencies.

One day, she found herself sitting in her car at 11 PM, finishing up "emergency" work for a client while missing her daughter's dance recital. That was her wake-up call.

Through our work together, Sarah started small. First, she set business hours for client communications. Then she practiced saying, "I'll check my calendar and get back to you," instead of automatic yeses. Within three months, she not only had her evenings back, but her clients actually respected her more.

"I thought setting boundaries would hurt my business," she told me. "Instead, it saved it—and my sanity."

LET'S BREAK DOWN THE B.R.A.V.E APPROACH TO UNDERSTANDING YOUR BOUNDARY STRUGGLES:

B - Boundaries: Identify where your current boundaries are fuzzy

> **Example 1:** You find yourself answering work emails at 10 PM "just this once" (which happens three times a week).
> **Example 2:** Your mother-in-law drops by unannounced because "she was in the neighborhood" (for the fifth time this month).
> **Ask yourself:** Where do you feel that pit in your stomach because you know someone's about to cross an invisible line?

R - Recognize patterns of when and why you say yes when you mean no

> **Example 1:** You volunteer for the PTA bake sale even

though you're already overwhelmed because "no one else will do it."

Example 2: You take on extra projects at work because you "don't want to seem uncooperative."

Pattern Check: Do you say yes more often when you're feeling guilty? Worried about disappointing others? Trying to prove your worth?

A - Authentic Action starts with understanding your true needs

Example 1: That yoga class you keep meaning to take but "never have time for" might actually be essential, not optional.

Example 2: Your need for quiet time in the morning isn't "being antisocial" - it's self-preservation!

Truth Talk: What do you actually want versus what you think you should want?

V - Validate your right to have limits (yes, even with family!)

Example 1: It's okay to say "We're not hosting Thanksgiving this year" without providing a 15-point justification.

Example 2: You can love your best friend AND not be available for her 2-hour daily drama download calls.

Remember: Your limits aren't up for democratic vote - even by people you love!

E - Evolve past the guilt of putting yourself first

Example 1: Booking a massage instead of attending your third baby shower this month isn't selfish - it's necessary.

Example 2: Taking a lunch break away from your desk

isn't "slacking" - it's maintaining your energy for better work.

Growth Check: Notice how much more you have to give when you're not running on empty!

One of my clients used this framework to transform her "always available" status at work. She started with one boundary: no meetings before 9 AM because she needed focused work time. The world didn't end, her productivity soared, and her team actually respected her more!

Remember: You're not being mean - you're being clear. You're not being selfish - you're being sensible. And you're definitely not alone in this journey!

Where Can You Set Boundaries? Everywhere!

- **Social Media**—No, you don't have to accept every friend request. Stop comparing yourself to every post you see.
- **Time**—Your calendar is not an all-you-can-book buffet. Be intentional and create time blocks just for you.
- **Energy**—You're not a 24/7 emotional support hotline. Stop allowing energy suckers to have all the access to you. Save some energy for yourself.
- **Space**—Your office isn't the neighborhood coffee shop. You are allowed to take up space!
- **Money**—Your wallet isn't a community resource. No is a complete sentence!

And With Whom? Everyone!

- **Family**—Even your mom, who "just wants what's best." If your family member doesn't have your best interests at heart, it might be time to love them from a distance.

Sometimes space and distance will make people understand how much they take advantage of you.

- **Friends**—Including the one who "really needs your help." Their needs are not more important than your own.
- **Coworkers**—Yes, even your boss. If you don't set boundaries here, how do you expect to have a personal life? Leave work at work.
- **That random person** who "just has a quick question." You are not here to take care of everyone!

Daily Affirmation: "My boundaries are not up for negotiation, and that's okay."

REFLECTION CORNER:

Pause here for a moment.

Ask yourself:

1. What's your biggest boundary struggle right now?
2. When was the last time you said yes but really wanted to say no?
3. What's the story you tell yourself about why you "can't" set boundaries?

Power Moves for Your Boundary Journey:

- Start with something small (like not checking work emails after 6 PM)
- Practice saying, "I'll need to check my calendar" instead of an immediate yes

Remember: Other people's reactions to your boundaries are about them, not you

B.R.A.V.E ACTION STEPS:

1. List three situations where you consistently override your own needs
2. Write down what you're afraid might happen if you set boundaries
3. Create one small, manageable boundary this week
4. Practice saying no to something minor daily
5. Celebrate each time you honor your boundaries (yes, even the tiny ones!)

Remember: Progress over perfection. You didn't learn to be a people-pleaser overnight, and you won't unlearn it overnight either. But each small step counts!

Quote to Keep Close:

Daring to set boundaries is about having the courage to love ourselves, even when we risk disappointing others.

— BRENÉ BROWN

---

3. Keeping Promises to Yourself

BOUNDARIES START WITHIN

You can't set strong boundaries with others until you honor the ones you set with yourself.

— UNKNOWN

Picture this: You finally carve out a Saturday afternoon just for you — to read, to recharge, maybe to nap. You've been dreaming about it all week. But then ... someone texts needing a "quick favor," or that to-do list taps you on the shoulder, and before you know it, your "me time" has vanished into thin air.

And the worst part?

You were the one who let it happen.

Ouch, right?

HERE'S THE TRUTH NO ONE TELLS YOU:

Boundaries aren't just about protecting yourself from other people. They start with protecting yourself ... from yourself. Setting boundaries with yourself is about keeping promises to YOU.

It's about saying, "I matter enough to honor my own needs, even when no one else is watching."

Why Self-Boundaries Are Non-Negotiable:

- They build your self-trust muscle.
- They make external boundary-setting feel natural (not terrifying).
- They teach you that your time, energy, and well-being are worth protecting — no permission slip needed.
- When you respect your own limits, it becomes so much easier to expect (and require) others to do the same.

Common Places Where We Break Boundaries with Ourselves:

- **Time:** Promising yourself a break ... and working through it anyway.
- **Energy:** Committing to rest ... then saying yes to "just one more thing."
- **Emotions:** Saying you'll process your feelings ... but numbing out with scrolling or busyness instead.
- **Health:** Committing to movement, water, sleep ... but abandoning it for "one more task."
- **Dreams:** Promising you'll work on that passion project ... and always putting it last.

Sound familiar?

(If your hand is in the air, you're not alone — I've been there too.)

One of my clients, Melissa, used to joke that she was "the queen of breaking dates with herself." She would plan self-care days, creative writing time, even just quiet mornings — and always cancel on herself first when someone else needed something.

Through our work together, Melissa realized something powerful: "If I don't take my time seriously, why would anyone else?" When she started honoring her own calendar like it was sacred, something magical happened:

Her confidence soared.

Her resentment faded.

Her relationships actually improved—because she wasn't pouring from an empty cup anymore.

HOW TO SET (AND KEEP) SELF-BOUNDARIES LIKE A B.R.A.V.E QUEEN

B - Boundaries With Yourself

Start by identifying one area where you consistently break promises to yourself.

- Maybe it's saying you'll go to bed earlier.
- Maybe it's saying you'll protect your Saturday mornings.
- Ask yourself: "Where am I telling myself 'later' when I actually mean 'never'?"

R - Recognize & Release the Sabotage Stories

Notice the sneaky stories you tell yourself:

- "It's not a big deal if I skip it."
- "I'll do it when things calm down."
- "Other people need me more."

Reality check: Your dreams, your energy, and your peace deserve to be prioritized — not constantly postponed.

A - Authentic Action (Small but Mighty)

Take one tiny authentic step today:

- Protect one 30-minute pocket of "you" time.
- Complete one small thing you've promised yourself.
- Say no to yourself when you're tempted to break that promise.

V - Validate & Value Your Effort

Celebrate every small promise you keep.

- 15 minutes of reading?
- 5 minutes of meditation?
- One glass of water before coffee?

It all counts. Keeping small promises builds massive self-trust.

E - Empower & Evolve

Each time you keep a promise to yourself, you evolve into the woman who doesn't need to explain her "no" — because she knows her worth.

Small wins turn into new standards.

New standards turn into a new identity.
And that identity? She's unstoppable.

Daily Affirmation:

"I am worthy of my time, my care, and my promises."

REFLECTION CORNER:

Pause here for a moment.

Ask yourself:

1. Where have I consistently broken promises to myself?
2. What's one small boundary with myself I can set this week?
3. How do I feel when I honor my own needs first?

B.R.A.V.E ACTION STEPS FOR THIS WEEK:

B - Choose one area where you'll set a boundary with yourself.
R - Write down the sabotage story you want to release.
A - Take one tiny action to honor that boundary today.
V - Celebrate keeping that promise — even if it feels small.
E - Evolve by tracking your boundary wins for the week.

Quote to Keep Close:

The relationship you have with yourself sets the tone for every relationship you have.

— UNKNOWN

PART TWO
Building Better Boundaries

Boundaries aren't about pushing people away — they're about standing close to yourself.

— JEN ANDERSON

Affirmation:

"Every time I set a boundary, I build a life that feels more like mine."

4. Sorry Not Sorry

THE ART OF GUILT-FREE BOUNDARY SETTING

No is a complete sentence.

— ANNE LAMOTT

Picture this: It's a Tuesday evening, and you're sitting in your car outside your house, taking deep breaths before going inside, because you know your family will ask why you can't host Thanksgiving this year. Sound familiar?

Here's the truth: I used to be the queen of the "Sorry, but..." club. Every boundary I set came with a side of apology and a main course of guilt. Until a moment that changed everything.

I recalls the exact moment my perspective on boundaries shifted. I was on a coaching call with a client, completely exhausted from back-to-back sessions, when she asked me a question that hit home: "Jen, you teach us about boundaries, but when was the last time you honored yours?"

Ouch. Talk about a wake-up call.

That night, I sat down and wrote out every time I'd said "sorry" that week for:

- Taking a lunch break
- Not answering texts immediately
- Wanting to spend a weekend alone
- Saying no to a volunteer opportunity

The list was longer than my weekly grocery list. And that's when it hit me: We don't need to apologize for having boundaries any more than we need to apologize for having a front door on our house.

Let's Break Down the Boundary Basics:

Rigid Boundaries vs. Healthy Boundaries

Think of it this way: Rigid boundaries are like wearing a suit of armor to a pool party—sure, nothing's getting in, but you're also not having any fun. Healthy boundaries are more like a good sports bra—supportive when you need it, flexible when you don't, and essential for comfort!

One of my favorite client transformations was with Rebecca, an executive who came to me saying, "I feel like I'm everyone's emergency contact." She was the go-to person for every crisis, every project, every emotional download.

Using the B.R.A.V.E method, we worked on building her boundary muscles:

B - Boundaries: She identified where her energy was leaking—The people who constantly came to her no matter what she had going on.

R - Recognize & Release: She spotted her people-pleasing patterns—why she always felt compelled to say "yes."

A - Authentic Action: She started with simple "no's"—"No, I don't want to go to lunch today."

V - Validate & Value: She celebrated each boundary win—learned to be proud of herself.

E - Empower & Evolve: She became confident in her choices—she trusted herself more and more with every choice.

Three months later, she told me: "For the first time in my life, I declined a project without offering three alternatives and my first-born child as compensation!"

Signs You're Rocking Your Boundaries:

- You can say "no" without writing a dissertation to explain why
- Your calendar isn't looking like a game of Tetris gone wrong
- You actually enjoy your free time instead of filling it with other people's emergencies
- Your energy tank isn't always running on empty

Signs You're Still in the Sorry Zone:

- Your go-to phrase is "I'm so sorry, but..."
- You feel guilty for taking a lunch break
- Your boundaries come with more footnotes than a research paper

- You're the human version of 911 for everyone else's problems

THE B.R.A.V.E BOUNDARY BUILDER WORKSHOP

(Complete these exercises over the next week.)

Day 1: Boundary Audit (B - Boundaries)

Get out your journal (or phone notes) and track for one full day:

- Every time you say "sorry" unnecessarily
- Every time you say "yes" but mean "no"
- Every situation that leaves you feeling drained
- Every time you over-explain your decisions

Pro Tip: Use my "Energy Traffic Light" system:
🌑 Green: Activities that energize you
🌑 Yellow: Activities that are neutral
🌑 Red: Activities that drain you

Day 2: Pattern Recognition (R - Recognize & Release)

The "Why Do I Say Yes?" Exercise: List your last 5 "reluctant yesses."
For each one, answer:

1. What was I afraid would happen if I said no?
2. What story am I telling myself about saying no?
3. What would I tell my best friend in this situation?

Day 3: Action Alignment (A - Authentic Action)

The "No Practice" Challenge:
Write down 3 different ways to say no:

- **Direct no:** "No, I won't be able to help with that project."
- **Alternative no:** "I can't do that, but here's what I can do..."
- **Future no:** "I'm not available for extra commitments right now."

Practice these in the mirror (I know it sounds silly, but trust me!)
Record yourself saying them on your phone
Listen back and notice: Do you sound apologetic? Confident? Uncertain?

Day 4: Value Validation (V - Validate & Value)

Create Your "Permission Slip" Portfolio:
Write yourself permission slips for common boundary situations:
"I give myself permission to..."

- Take a lunch break without my phone
- Say no without explaining why
- Leave the group chat that drains me
- Decline last-minute plans

Day 5: Empowerment Evolution (E - Empower & Evolve)

The "Boundary Success Log":
Create a special section in your journal for:

- Boundary wins (no matter how small!)
- Positive outcomes from setting boundaries
- Unexpected benefits of saying no
- Proud moments of standing firm

Bonus Exercise: The "Sorry Swap"

Replace these common apologetic phrases with empowered ones:
Instead of: "I'm sorry, but I can't make it."
Use: "Thank you for thinking of me. I won't be able to attend."

Instead of: "Sorry for taking so long to respond..."
Use: "Thank you for your patience."

Instead of: "Sorry to bother you, but..."
Use: "I'd like to discuss something with you."

WEEKLY CHALLENGE: THE B.R.A.V.E BOUNDARY BINGO

Said no without apologizing	Paused before making a decision	Prioritized self-care	Took a full lunch break
Declined a non-essential meeting	Didn't explain a "no"	Set a time boundary	Let a call go to voicemail
Didn't over-explain	Free space: Self-high five!	Used "I" statements	Celebrated a boundary win

www.thankfulheartscoaching.com

Remember: Progress isn't linear. Some days you'll rock your boundaries, others you'll slip back into old patterns. That's okay!

What matters is that you keep practicing. Try to get 4 in a row by the end of the week, or fill the whole card if you're feeling bold!

Daily Affirmation:

"My boundaries are not up for debate, and that's perfectly okay."

Reflection Corner:

Pause here for a moment.

Ask yourself:

1. What's your most common boundary apology?
2. If your boundaries could talk, what would they say they need?
3. What's one boundary you can practice setting this week without saying sorry?

B.R.A.V.E Action Steps:

B - Boundaries

Complete the "Boundary Blueprint" exercise:

1. Draw three circles labeled "Non-negotiable," "Flexible," and "Growth Edge"
2. List your boundaries in each circle
3. Start with one boundary from your "Growth Edge" to practice this week
4. • Create your "Not To-Do List"-things you're no longer saying yes to

R - Recognize & Release

Track your "sorry" statements for 3 days

- Identify your top 3 guilt triggers around boundaries
- Write a "permission letter" to yourself, releasing the need to explain your boundaries
- Notice which relationships trigger the most boundary anxiety

A - Authentic Action

Practice these three boundary statements daily:

- "That doesn't work for me."
- "I've made my decision."
- "I need time to think about it."

Choose one small boundary to set this week (like taking an uninterrupted lunch break).
Use "I" statements when communicating your needs.

V - Validate & Value

Create a "Boundary Win" journal entry each night.

1. Write down three ways your boundaries protect your energy.
2. List the positive outcomes you've experienced from setting boundaries.
3. Celebrate small wins in our Blissful Besties community.

E - Empower & Evolve

- Share your boundary success story (even tiny ones count!).
- Help another member of our community validate their boundary-setting journey.

- Plan your next boundary upgrade (what's your next growth edge?).
- Create a go-to phrase for reinforcing boundaries when challenged.

Remember: Transformation happens one small step at a time. Choose one action from each category to focus on this week.

Weekly Check-In Questions:

1. Which boundary did I maintain successfully?
2. Where did I feel challenged?
3. What support do I need to stay consistent?
4. How did it feel to prioritize my needs?

Building Your Boundary Toolkit—Without the Guilt!

Let me share another quick story. Last month, during our Blissful Besties group call, one of our members shared how she finally told her mother-in-law that Sunday dinners needed to be every other week instead of weekly. "I felt like I was going to pass out," she laughed, "but you know what? The world didn't end, and I got my Sundays back!"

That's the thing about boundaries - they feel terrifying until they feel terrific.

Let's Break Down How to Build Those Boundary Muscles:

Step 1: Get Crystal Clear (No More Fuzzy Lines!)

Remember playing Red Light, Green Light as a kid? Your boundaries need to be that clear. Pull out your journal (or your phone notes if you're like me and can never find a pen), and answer:

What makes you feel:

Energized (Green Light)
Cautious (Yellow Light)
Completely drained (Red Light)

Pro Tip: I have my clients keep a "boundary journal" for a week. Every time they feel resentful or exhausted, it's usually a sign that a boundary needs to be set.

Step 2: Communication Station (Without the Explanation Marathon)

Here's where most of us trip up - we think we need to write a novel explaining our boundaries. Spoiler alert: You don't!

Instead of: "I'm so sorry, but I can't make it to the committee meeting because my dog needs to be fed, and I have this thing, and my aunt's cousin's neighbor..."

Try: "I won't be able to attend the committee meeting. Thank you for understanding."

mic drop!!

Pro Tip: When you thank someone instead of apologizing, you put the focus back on them and stop making it all about you. This allows people to feel acknowledged instead of being passed over for all the other things you are apologizing to them about.

Step 3: The Pushback Plan

Let's be real - not everyone's going to do a happy dance when you set boundaries. Some people might push back harder than a toddler refusing bedtime.

Here's your game plan:

- Stay calm (even if you're screaming internally)
- Repeat your boundary (like a broken record)
- Remember: Their reaction is about them, not you

Real Talk Moment: One of my clients told me she lost three "friends" when she started setting boundaries. Know what she said? "Turns out they weren't friends - they were just used to me being their personal assistant!"

B.R.A.V.E Boundary Scripts to Keep in Your Back Pocket:

For Time Vampires:

"I've committed that time to other priorities."
(Notice: No sorry, no explanation needed!)

For Energy Drainers:

"I need to recharge right now. Let's connect next week."
(Setting a future connection keeps relationships intact while protecting your energy)

For The Guilt-Trippers:

"I understand you're disappointed, but my decision stands."
(Kind but firm - you're not responsible for managing their feelings)

Your Boundary-Setting Emergency Kit:

- Deep breathing (because sometimes saying no makes us forget to breathe)

- A list of pre-written responses (for when your brain goes blank)
- A support squad (people who cheer when you say no)
- Permission slips (yes, I actually give these to my clients!)

Daily Affirmation:

"Every boundary I set is an act of self-respect."

Power Moves for Your Journey:

- Start small—rather than immediately telling your boss to stop texting you at midnight, begin by waiting to reply until the next morning when you're at your desk at work.
- Practice in the mirror (seriously, it helps!)
- Celebrate your wins (did you say no to that extra project? That deserves a high-five!)

Remember: Progress over perfection. Some days you'll be a boundary-setting superhero, other days you'll say yes to three things you meant to say no to. It's all part of the journey.

Quote to Keep Close:

Every time you say yes to something you don't want to do, you're actually saying no to yourself.

B.R.A.V.E Action Steps for This Week:

Identify one boundary you need to set (start small!).

1. Write it down without apologies.
2. Practice saying it out loud.

3. Set the boundary.
4. Reward yourself for being brave.

Your Homework (Because Growth Happens in the Doing):

- Track your energy levels for one week.
- Note when you say yes but want to say no.
- Practice one boundary statement daily.
- Share your wins in our Blissful Besties community!

Remember: You're not being mean, you're being clear. You're not being selfish, you're being smart. And you're definitely not alone - we're all learning this together!

5. Standing Your Ground
(WITHOUT FEELING LIKE A MEANIE)

Boundaries are like your favorite pair of jeans - they only work if you actually wear them.

— UNKNOWN

Picture this: You've just set a beautiful boundary (yay you!), feeling all proud and empowered ... and then your mom calls asking why you won't host Easter dinner for the 47th year in a row. Your stomach drops, your throat gets tight, and suddenly you're wondering if boundaries are really worth all this drama.

Here's the truth: Setting boundaries is like buying a gym membership - it's a great first step, but the real work happens when you show up to use it.

Let me share something that happened in my journey. Last year, I set a firm "no work calls after 6 PM" boundary. Easy, right? Well, one evening, a long-time client called at 8 PM with an "emergency." My finger hovered over the "accept" button as my people-pleasing programming kicked in. But instead of answering, I took a deep breath and sent a text: "I see you called. I'm available tomorrow at 10 AM for any urgent matters."

You know what happened? The world didn't end. In fact, the next day, my client apologized for calling late and respected my boundary from then on.

LET'S BREAK DOWN THE B.R.A.V.E WAY TO ENFORCE THOSE BOUNDARIES:

B - Boundaries in Action

- Clear is kind (thanks, Brené Brown!)
- Consistency is key
- Calm is your superpower

Sarah struggled with her mother-in-law's daily unannounced visits. Using our B.R.A.V.E method, she transformed from anxious door-answerer to confident boundary-keeper.

R - Recognize & Release

- Identified her fear of being seen as "mean"
- Released the guilt about needing personal space
- Recognized her right to a peaceful home

A - Authentic Action

She started with: "We love seeing you, but we need advance notice. How about we set up regular Tuesday coffee dates instead?"

V - Validate & Value

Celebrated small wins: "I maintained my boundary today without apologizing!"

E - Empower & Evolve

Three months later, she had a better relationship with her mother-in-law and her sanity intact!

Your Boundary Enforcement Toolkit:

The Broken Record, Without Breaking Your Spirit

Instead of: Explaining, defending, debating, try: calm, consistent repetition

Example:

Them: "But why can't you help? You always help!"
You: "I'm not available to help this time."

Them: "But it'll only take a minute!"
You: "I'm not available to help this time."
(Notice: No explanations needed!)

The Redirect—Like a Traffic Cop for Conversations

When someone crosses your conversational boundaries:

- "Let's focus on something more positive..."
- "I'd love to hear about your vacation instead!"

- "How about we talk about that new coffee shop?"

The Exit Strategy—Your Get-Out-Of-Guilt-Free Card

Have these ready:

- "I need to wrap this up now."
- "Thanks for understanding!"
- "Let's pick this up another time."

Daily Affirmation:

"My boundaries are not up for negotiation, and that's healthy!"

B.R.A.V.E ACTION STEPS FOR ENFORCING BOUNDARIES:

B - Build Your Response Arsenal

Create 3 go-to phrases for common boundary pushers:

- For the guilt-trippers: "I know this isn't the answer you wanted, but my decision stands."
- For the persistent pushers: "I've made my choice, and I'm at peace with it."
- For the emergency-makers: "I can help tomorrow during regular hours."

R - Reinforce Without Remorse

Practice the "No Apology Challenge":

- Catch yourself before saying "sorry."

- Replace "sorry, but..." with "I've decided..."
- Keep a "Victory Log" of successful boundary moments.

A - Act With Authority

Choose one boundary to enforce firmly this week

1. Use the "pause and respond" technique:
2. Take a breath.
3. Remember your worth.
4. Respond with confidence.
5. Celebrate each time you stand your ground.

V - Value Your Voice

- Record yourself saying your boundaries (yes, really!).
- Listen for apologetic tones or uncertainty.
- Practice until you hear confidence.
- Share your wins in our Blissful Besties community.

E - Evolve Your Enforcement

- Start small, build big.
- Track your progress.
- Adjust as needed.
- Keep what works.

Remember: Other people's reactions to your boundaries are about them, not you!

Practical Power Moves:

The Three-Strike Rule

- First time: Gentle reminder
- Second time: Clear restatement
- Third time: Consequence time

The Energy Preservation Plan

- Identify your boundary-pushing triggers.
- Create an exit strategy for each.
- Practice your responses.
- Have a self-care plan ready.

The Support Squad Protocol

- Share your boundaries with trusted allies.
- Ask for specific support.
- Celebrate wins together.
- Learn from setbacks.

Daily Check-In Questions:

- Did I maintain my boundaries today?
- Where did I feel strongest?
- What could I do differently tomorrow?
- What win can I celebrate?

Remember: Progress over perfection. Some days you'll be a boundary-enforcing superhero, other days not so much. It's all part of the journey!

Quote to Keep Close:

Every time you uphold a boundary, you're teaching people how to treat you.

Your Homework (Because Growth Happens in Practice):

1. Pick one boundary to focus on this week.
2. Write down three ways you'll enforce it.
3. Practice your responses in the mirror.
4. Share your experience in our next Blissful Besties call!

Pro Tip: Keep a "Boundary Victory Journal" - even small wins count!

CHAPTER SUMMARY:

Enforcing boundaries doesn't make you mean; it makes you clear. Instead of driving people away, it invites them to connect with the real you. Most importantly, it's not about perfection, but a commitment to progress.

Think of boundary enforcement like training a puppy - consistency is key, rewards work better than punishment, and sometimes you need to clean up a few messes along the way!

Next time someone pushes back on your boundaries, remember: You're not being difficult, you're being deliberate. You're not being selfish, you're being self-aware. And you're definitely not alone - we're all learning this together!

Ready to put these tools into practice? Start with one small boundary today. Remember, every journey starts with a single step, or in this case, a single "no"!

6. The Boundary Bonus

WHY BEING 'SELFISH' ACTUALLY MAKES YOU A BETTER HUMAN

Setting boundaries is self-care, not selfishness.

Picture this: You've just said no to hosting yet another family dinner (gasp!), and your inner people-pleaser is having a full-blown meltdown. But wait... is that a strange feeling of peace creeping in?

Let me share something that happened in my journey. Last month, I declined three "quick coffee chats" that would have eaten up my prep time for an event I was getting ready to lead. The old me would have squeezed them in, shown up frazzled or unprepared to the event, and resented every minute spent having "coffee." Instead, I felt something magical: Relief. Energy. Presence.

THE BOUNDARY BENEFITS BUNDLE: WHY SETTING LIMITS MAKES LIFE JUICIER

The "No More Nonsense" Superpower

Remember when you would say yes to every request, even if it meant sacrificing your own sanity? Those days are officially over!

When you set boundaries, you get to:

- Choose where your energy goes.
- Skip the drama that doesn't serve you.
- Actually enjoy your own life (shocking, I know!).

Lisa was tired of dating men who seemed like a good fit for her, only to find out six months in that one had expectations for her to "mother" him. After digging into the story, it turns out that Lisa, because of her kind heart and genuine desire to be helpful, was really showing these men how to treat her. They learned she would do everything for them, and they let her. This caused her to resent them and eventually forced a breakup. After implementing her B.R.A.V.E boundaries, she told me: "For the first time in my relationship, I get to have an opinion on things; we do things I want to do, and we do them together. It's not just me doing everything alone or for them. It's so amazing to have a true partner!"

The Energy Protection Plan

Think of your energy like your phone battery:

- Without boundaries: 10% by 10 AM
- With boundaries: Fully charged and ready to rock

The Resentment Reducer

You know that bubbling feeling of frustration when you've said yes to something you really wanted to say "no" to? That's your boundary alarm system going off!

B.R.A.V.E BENEFITS BREAKDOWN:

B - Boundaries Create Freedom

- More time for what matters.
- Less stress about saying no.
- Clear expectations for everyone.

R - Recognize & Release the Good Stuff

- Less guilt, more joy.
- Fewer obligations, more opportunities.
- Less people-pleasing, more self-pleasing.

A - Authentic Action Unleashed

- Your relationships get real—bye-bye fake friendships!
- Your yes means YES—not "ugh, I guess..."
- Your time becomes actually yours.

Maria used to volunteer for every PTA committee until she was running on empty. After setting boundaries, she told me, "I now chair ONE committee I'm passionate about, and I do a better job than when I was spread thin across five!"

Your value increases when you focus your energy instead of spreading it too thin in different areas.

V - Value Skyrockets

- Your self-respect grows.
- Others treat you with more respect.
- Your time becomes more valuable (funny how that works!).

E - Evolution in Action

- Toxic relationships naturally fade away.
- Healthy relationships flourish.
- Your career actually improves (plot twist!).

THE CAREER CONNECTION

Let's talk about how boundaries make you a workplace superhero:

- No more answering emails at midnight.
- Actually taking your lunch break.
- Learning to say "that's not in my scope" without guilt.

When I first started Thankful Hearts Coaching, I said yes to every time slot clients requested. 6 AM calls? Sure! 9 PM sessions? Why not? I was exhausted, cranky, and definitely not showing up as my best self. Setting business hours wasn't just good for me - it made me a better coach for my clients.

THE RELATIONSHIP REVOLUTION

Here's the magic: When you set boundaries, you actually become MORE available for the people and things that matter. It's like decluttering your house - suddenly you can find everything you need!

Your Boundary Benefits Checklist:

√ More energy for what matters.
√ Better relationships (the real ones stick around!).
√ Clearer mind, calmer heart.
√ Time for self-care without guilt.
√ Professional growth (because burned-out isn't a career goal).

Remember: Every boundary you set is like making a deposit in your self-worth bank account. The interest? Pure joy!

Daily Affirmation:

"My boundaries create space for magic to happen."

B.R.A.V.E Action Steps:

1. List three ways boundaries have already improved your life.
2. Notice where you feel more energized.
3. Celebrate one relationship that's grown stronger.
4. Share your wins in our Blissful Besties community!

   Pro Tip: Use a "Boundary Benefits Journal" - when guilt creeps in, read through your wins!

CHAPTER SUMMARY:

Setting boundaries isn't just about saying no - it's about saying yes to yourself. It's not about building walls - it's about creating space for what truly matters. And most importantly, it's not about being selfish - it's about being sustainable.

Remember: You can't pour from an empty cup, and you definitely can't change the world if you're too exhausted to get off the couch!

Ready to enjoy these benefits? Start with one small boundary today. Your future self will thank you (probably while enjoying a peaceful cup of coffee that's still hot)!

7. The Digital Dilemma

SETTING BOUNDARIES WITH TECHNOLOGY

You are not obligated to be available 24/7 — to anyone, including your phone.

— UNKNOWN

We live in a world where being "reachable" is often mistaken for being "responsible." The pressure to respond instantly, stay connected, and always be available has quietly crept into our everyday routines — often without us even noticing. At some point, our devices stopped being tools *we* use and started becoming tools that *use us*. This chapter isn't about blaming technology. It's about recognizing how digital overload quietly drains our time, energy, and presence — and learning how to take that power back with compassion, clarity, and firm boundaries.

Picture this:

You finally sit down for a quiet moment — coffee in hand, favorite chair, a few precious minutes to yourself.

Then... the notifications start.

A text here.

An email ping there.

A social media comment you "should" answer.

Before you know it, your peaceful moment has been swallowed whole by the tiny, glowing rectangle in your hand.

Here's the truth:

In today's world, technology isn't just a convenience. it's a boundary-pusher. Unless you intentionally limit your digital life, daily interruptions will hijack your peace, energy, and focus.

Technology boundaries aren't about abandoning your devices. They're about reclaiming your attention, your presence, and your right to disconnect without guilt.

Why Technology Boundaries Matter More Than Ever

Constant Access = Constant Drain:

Without boundaries, you're giving away your time and energy one ping at a time.

Urgency Addiction:

When everyone expects an instant reply, you live in reaction mode, not creation mode.

Comparison Culture:

Social media often feeds insecurity, urgency, and false expectations — unless you manage it mindfully.

Invisible Overwhelm:

You may not feel busy, but a cluttered digital space clutters your mind.

Protecting your digital space is as essential as protecting your physical space.

It's not optional self-care. It's survival.

THE B.R.A.V.E DIGITAL BOUNDARY PLAN

B - Begin with Awareness

Notice where technology eats into your time and energy the most.

- Endless scrolling?
- Text threads that never end?
- Responding to work emails at 9 PM?

Make a quick list today. Where are your phone, laptop, and notifications stealing peace from you?

R - Recognize Your Triggers

When do you reach for your device without thinking?

- Boredom
- Loneliness
- Stress
- Fear of missing out (FOMO)

Recognizing the emotional trigger gives you the power to choose differently.

A - Authentic Action to Reclaim Your Power

Set one small but clear tech boundary this week. Examples:

- No phone the first 30 minutes after I wake up.
- No email after 6 PM.
- Social media-free Sundays.
- Turn off notifications except from key people.

Small digital shifts create huge emotional shifts.

V - Validate Your Right to Disconnect

Give yourself permission to:

- Let a text sit unanswered overnight.
- Reply to emails during business hours only.
- Take social media breaks without announcements or apologies.
- Protect your attention like the precious resource it is.
- Validation starts with reminding yourself: "My availability is a gift I choose to give — not an obligation."

E - Evolve as Needed

Technology changes. Life seasons change. Your boundaries can and should evolve too.

Maybe right now you need strong boundaries around work emails. Later, you may need boundaries around group texts or online news consumption.

Adjust as needed — no guilt required.

Daily Affirmation

"I protect my time, energy, and peace — online and offline."

REFLECTION CORNER

Pause here for a moment.

Ask yourself:

1. What area of my digital life drains me the most right now?
2. When do I feel my energy dip after interacting with my devices?
3. What story am I telling myself about needing to be "always available"?
4. What small shift can I make this week to reclaim my digital peace?

B.R.A.V.E ACTION STEPS FOR THIS WEEK

B - Begin

Identify one tech boundary you want to set.

R - Recognize

Notice when the urge to check or reply immediately arises.

A - Act

Implement one digital boundary today — no need to wait for Monday.

V - Validate

Celebrate when you honor your tech boundary, even once.

E - Evolve

Adjust the boundary as you notice what works best for you.

PRACTICAL EXAMPLES OF TECHNOLOGY BOUNDARIES

Work Boundaries

- No checking work email after 6 PM.
- Turning off Slack notifications during lunch.
- Setting an "out of office" auto-response when you're truly unavailable.

Social Media Boundaries

- Unfollow accounts that trigger comparison or negativity.
- Take weekends off social apps.
- Move social media apps off your home screen.

Text & Call Boundaries

- Setting a "phone-free" hour each evening.
- Turning your phone to Do Not Disturb after 8 PM.
- Creating custom text responses like, "I'll respond tomorrow when I'm available."

Entertainment Boundaries

- No binge-watching shows on work nights.

- 30-minute maximum YouTube or TikTok scroll time.

Quote to Keep Close:

You're allowed to be unavailable, protect your peace, and live beyond the reach of a notification.

— UNKNOWN

---

8. When Your Boundaries Have Backlash

HANDLING THE PUSHBACK LIKE A PRO

A boundary is not a wall, it's a door you get to choose when to open.

— UNKNOWN

P icture this: You've finally gathered the courage to tell your sister you can't be her on-call babysitter anymore, and suddenly you're the "bad guy" at every family gathering. Sound familiar?

Let me share something that hit close to home. Last year, I faced major pushback when I stopped being the "emergency counselor" for everyone in my circle. Friends would text at all hours with their latest crisis, expecting immediate support and advice. The people-pleaser in me felt terrible saying, "This needs to wait until our next scheduled chat." However, I knew I had to protect my energy to show up fully for my coaching clients.

The first few weeks were rough - there were guilt trips, passive-aggressive messages, and even a few "you've changed" comments. But here's what actually happened when I held firm: The loyal friends adjusted and started respecting my boundaries, while others naturally drifted away. The unexpected bonus? My advice became more valuable because it came from a well-rested, fully present version of me.

LET'S BREAK DOWN THE B.R.A.V.E WAY TO HANDLE BOUNDARY BACKLASH

B - Boundaries Under Pressure

Common Pushback You Might Face:

- "But you always help!"
- "I thought we were friends..."
- "You've changed" (Yes, that's the point!)

One of my clients, Jennifer, faced massive resistance when she stopped being the family's default holiday host. "The guilt trips were Olympic-level," she laughed. "But once I stood firm, something amazing happened - my cousins started taking turns hosting, and I actually got to enjoy holidays again!"

R - Recognize & Release

Recognize the manipulation tactics:

- Guilt trips
- Silent treatment
- "Just this once," promises–release the responsibility for others' reactions

A - Authentic Action

Standing Your Ground Without Becoming a Fortress:

- Use "I" statements
- Keep responses simple
- Stay calm (even if you're screaming internally)

V - Validate & Value

Remember:

- Your needs are valid.
- Your time is valuable.
- Your peace is priceless.

E - Empower & Evolve

Growth Signs to Celebrate:

- Saying no without a three-page explanation.
- Feeling peaceful instead of guilty.
- Watching others adjust to your new standards.

COMMON BOUNDARY CHALLENGES (AND HOW TO ROCK THEM)

The Fear Factor

"But what if they don't like me anymore?"

Here's the truth

People who only like you when you're exhausting yourself for them don't actually like YOU - they like your services.

The Guilt Game

When your inner critic starts the "but you should..." soundtrack, remember: You're not being selfish, you're being sustainable.

The Clarity Confusion

Not sure where to draw the line? Start with this question: "Would I want someone I love treating themselves this way?"

The People-Pleaser Panic

My client Sarah used to say yes to every overtime request at work. Using our B.R.A.V.E method, she learned to say, "I can take this on tomorrow during regular hours," instead of, "Sorry, I'll do it right now!"

Your Boundary Protection Toolkit:

Scripts for Success:

- "That doesn't work for me."
- "I'll need to check my calendar."
- "I'm not available for that."

(Notice: No apologies needed!)

Emergency Response Kit:

- Deep breathing
- Pre-written responses
- Support squad on speed dial

Self-Care Safety Net:

- Regular check-ins with yourself
- Celebration of small wins

- Permission to adjust as needed

Daily Affirmation:

"Other people's reactions to my boundaries are not my responsibility."

B.R.A.V.E ACTION STEPS

1. Identify your top three boundary challenges.
2. Create response scripts for each.
3. Practice in the mirror (yes, really!).
4. Share your progress—you never know who else you will inspire.

Remember: Progress over perfection. Some days you'll handle pushback like a pro; other days you'll need to regroup and try again. Both are perfectly okay!

Quote to Keep Close:

Your boundaries are the bridge between who you were and who you are becoming.

— JEN ANDERSON

PARTING THOUGHTS

Handling boundary resistance isn't about being perfect - it's about being persistent. Every time you stand firm in your boundaries, you're not just protecting your peace - you're teaching others how to respect it.

Ready to handle the pushback like a pro? Start with one small boundary today. Remember, you've got this, and more importantly, you've got an entire community of boundary-setting sisters cheering you on!

9. Bouncing Back & Holding Strong

REPAIRING BROKEN BOUNDARIES AND CRISIS-PROOFING YOUR LIFE

Boundaries aren't about being perfect. They're about being persistent.

— JEN ANDERSON

Let's get one thing straight: breaking a boundary doesn't mean you're broken. It means you're in the middle of real, gritty human growth. Boundaries are like any other life-changing practice — they come with wins, setbacks, and moments where your old habits sneak back in, disguised in new ways. This chapter isn't about perfection. It's about what you do *after* the backslide. It's about bouncing back, holding strong, and knowing that every time you reset, you're actually reinforcing your strength. Repair is not weakness — it's wisdom. This is how you build resilience!

You set the boundary.

You felt strong.

You even had the perfect script ready.

And then ... life happened.

Or emotions happened.

Or guilt snuck back in.

And somehow, you ended up doing the very thing you promised you wouldn't.

If you're nodding along right now, exhale with me.

You're not failing. You're growing.

Real boundaries aren't a one-and-done event. They're a living, breathing practice.

And sometimes? That practice gets messy.

This chapter is about what happens when things don't go perfectly — and how to keep going without shame, blame, or giving up.

When You Break Your Own Boundary

Maybe you said yes to something you meant to say no to.

Maybe you let a pushy person wear you down.

Maybe you stayed too long in a conversation, a project, or a space you knew wasn't honoring you.

It happens. It will happen. And it does not mean you aren't strong enough for this work.

It simply means you're human.

Here's the truth:

You can repair a broken boundary — just like you can reset a healthy habit after slipping up.

The most important part?

Don't turn a slip into a spiral.

THE B.R.A.V.E BOUNCE-BACK METHOD

B - Boundaries Are a Practice, Not a Perfection Project

- Stop expecting yourself to set a boundary once and have it stick forever.
- Boundaries are muscles. You build them through use, not theory.
- Each stumble is actually a rep.

R - Recognize the Slippery Moment

- When did it happen? What pulled you off course?
- Was it guilt? Pressure? Fear? Fatigue?
- Get curious — not critical.
- Awareness is power.

A - Authentic Repair Action

- Own it quickly. Reset clearly.
- You don't need a lengthy apology or an explanation to others.
- You just need to realign with yourself.

Example:

"I realize I agreed to something that doesn't actually work for me. I need to update that commitment."

V - Validate Your Growth

Slipping doesn't erase the progress you've made. One backslide doesn't cancel out a dozen brave choices.

Every reset is evidence that you are committed to yourself.

E - Evolve Your Strategy

Ask yourself:

1. What support would have helped me hold the line?
2. What script could I have had ready?
3. What sign will I look for next time?
4. Adjust. Strengthen. Move forward.

WHEN LIFE GETS MESSY: EMERGENCY BOUNDARIES 101

Sometimes boundary work isn't about a calendar conflict or a minor guilt trip. Sometimes, life drops a crisis at your feet: divorce, grief, illness, caregiving, addiction in the family, job loss.

In these seasons, you need Emergency Boundaries—boundaries that are faster, firmer, and even more unapologetic.

Emergency Boundaries sound like:

- "I'm not available for that right now."
- "I can only take on the essentials this month."
- "I need to step away for my health and well-being."
- "I won't be discussing that."

In a crisis, your energy is a precious, limited resource.

- You're allowed:
- Ration it with care.
- Make survival your priority.

Be unapologetic about protecting your mental health.

One of my clients, Rachel, experienced this firsthand when she was navigating a sudden health diagnosis. Before her diagnosis, she struggled to say no to family obligations. Afterward, she became laser-focused:

"If it doesn't nourish me, it doesn't get my time."

The result? She not only protected her energy but also deepened the quality of the relationships that truly mattered.

Your crisis boundary might feel "harsh" at first. It's not. It's necessary.

This is not the season for gentle negotiating. This is the season for fiercely protecting your well-being.

Daily Affirmation

"I have the right to protect my peace, even when life gets messy."

REFLECTION CORNER

Pause here for a moment.

Ask yourself:

1. Where have I given myself grace after slipping up?
2. What story have I told myself about failing at boundaries?
3. How can I reframe a boundary slip as a success in awareness and growth?
4. Where might I need an Emergency Boundary in my current life season?

B.R.A.V.E ACTION STEPS FOR THIS WEEK

B - Begin by Owning One Slip

Think of a recent boundary you bent or broke. Write it down without judgment. Simply observe.

R - Recognize the Trigger

What caused you to compromise your boundary? Guilt? Exhaustion? Lack of a plan?

A - Authentic Repair Action

Choose one small, clear action to realign today.

V - Validate Your Growth

Identify three ways you've grown since starting this boundary journey.

E - Evolve for the Next Time

Draft a stronger, simpler boundary script you can use if this situation comes up again.

Quote to Keep Close

You haven't failed. You've discovered one more way to rise stronger.

— JEN ANDERSON

PART THREE
Living a Boundaried Life

When boundaries become a way of life, peace stops feeling like a luxury and starts feeling like your baseline."

— JEN ANDERSON

Affirmation:

"I lead with clarity, protect my energy, and create a life that reflects my deepest values."

10. The Boundary Butterfly Effect

HOW SMALL LIMITS CREATE BIG MAGIC

Small shifts in boundaries today create massive transformations tomorrow.

— JEN ANDERSON

Last month during our Blissful Besties group call, something beautiful happened. As one member shared how her "no" to taking on a work project had created space for a new hobby, another chimed in about finally taking art classes after decades of putting everyone else first. That's when it hit me - boundaries aren't just daily decisions, they're legacy builders.

THE B.R.A.V.E WAY

Your Boundaries Shape Your Future:

B - Boundaries Become Your Blueprint

Today's "no" becomes tomorrow's:

- Peace of mind
- Respected space
- Clear expectations

One of my Empowered & Aligned clients (let's call her Rachel) started with one tiny boundary: no phone during dinner. Six months later, she told me: "That one boundary sparked a revolution. My kids now know mom's attention is precious, my husband and I actually talk ... and somehow, I'm sleeping better!"

R - Recognize & Release the Ripple Effect

When you maintain healthy boundaries:

- Your kids learn self-respect.
- Your friends value your time more.
- Your colleagues respect your limits.
- Your family dynamics shift.

A - Authentic Action Creates Lasting Change

The magic happens when:

- Your yes means YES.
- Your no means NO.
- Your maybe means "I'll check my calendar."

V - Value Compounds Over Time

Just like a savings account, every boundary you set:

- Builds emotional wealth
- Grows relationship equity
- Increases your self-worth interest rate

E - Empower & Evolve for Generations

Your boundaries teach others:

- How to treat you
- What healthy relationships look like
- That self-care isn't selfish

THE LONG-TERM BOUNDARY BENEFITS BUNDLE

Emotional Resilience—AKA Your Superhero Cape

- Less people-pleasing panic
- More genuine connections
- Stronger sense of self

Mental Clarity (Brain Fog Be Gone!)

- Clearer decision-making
- Reduced overthinking
- More creative energy

Relationship Revolution

- Deeper connections
- Less resentment
- More authentic friendships

Physical Health Boost

- Better sleep—because you're not up worrying about saying no
- More energy—because you're not exhausted from saying yes
- Less stress-related issues

Career Catapult

- Increased respect at work
- Better work-life balance
- More meaningful contributions

THE GENERATIONAL GIFT

Here's the beautiful truth: Every boundary you set today creates a ripple effect for generations to come. When you show your daughter it's okay to say no, you're changing her future. When you lead with self-respect, you transform the workplace culture.

Daily Affirmation:

"My boundaries today create freedom for tomorrow."

B.R.A.V.E ACTION STEPS:

1. Notice one positive change from a boundary you've set.
2. Document the ripple effects.
3. Celebrate the small wins.
4. Share your legacy vision in our community.

Remember: Progress over perfection. Every tiny boundary you set is like planting a seed - it might not look like much today, but just wait until it blooms!

Your Boundary Legacy Checklist:

✓ Less stress, more joy

✓ Better relationships

✓ Clearer decisions

✓ Stronger self-trust

✓ More authentic life

PARTING THOUGHTS

Setting boundaries isn't just about protecting your peace today - it's about creating a legacy of self-respect that ripples through generations. Every time you honor your limits, you're not just changing your life - you're changing the world, one boundary at a time.

Ready to start your boundary legacy? Remember: The best time to set a boundary was yesterday. The second best time is now.

11. Boundary Myths Busted

WHAT THEY REALLY ARE (AND AREN'T!)

The biggest myth about boundaries is that they push people away. In reality, they show people exactly how to stay.

— UNKNOWN

During a recent Blissful Besties call, one of our members confessed, "I always thought boundaries meant being mean!" She had spent years saying yes to everything, worried that setting limits would make her the "bad guy." Sound familiar? Let's bust these boundary myths wide open!

THE B.R.A.V.E WAY TO UNDERSTANDING BOUNDARIES

B - Boundaries: What They Really Are

Myth: "Boundaries are walls to keep people out."

Truth:

- They're bridges to better relationships!
- They're guidelines, not guillotines
- They're self-care, not selfishness
- They're respect-builders, not relationship-wreckers

Amy feared setting boundaries would ruin her reputation as the 'helpful one' at work. Using our B.R.A.V.E method, she learned to say, "I can help with that tomorrow during work hours." The result? Her colleagues actually respected her more!

R - Recognize & Release These Myths:

Myth #1: "Boundaries are about controlling others."
Truth: They're about controlling your own energy and space.

Myth #2: "Setting boundaries is selfish."
Truth: It's like putting on your own oxygen mask first - you can't help others if you're suffocating!

A - Authentic Action vs. Common Misconceptions

Myth: "Boundaries must be aggressive."

Truth: They can be gentle, yet firm.
Example: Instead of, "Stop calling me all the time!"
Try: "I'm available for calls between 2-4 PM."

V - Validate & Value the Truth About Boundaries

Boundaries are:

- Flexible, not rigid
- Personal, not universal
- Evolving, not fixed

E - Empower & Evolve Beyond the Myths

Remember:

- Boundaries aren't about being mean
- They're not just about saying no
- They don't need to be perfect

TOP 10 BOUNDARY MYTHS BUSTED

"Boundaries push people away."
Truth: They actually show people how to stay close in a healthy way!

"Once set, they're set in stone."
Reality Check: Your boundaries can flex and grow with you.

"They're only for toxic relationships."
Nope: Even the healthiest relationships need them.

"Setting boundaries means you're high maintenance."
Actually, it means you're high value!

"They're just about saying No."
Truth: They're about saying yes to yourself first.
"Everyone should have the same boundaries."
Reality: Your boundaries are as unique as you are.

"They have to be dramatic."
Fact: The best boundaries are often quiet and consistent.

"Good people don't need them."
Truth: Good people need them most!

"They're only about words."
Reality: Actions set boundaries too!

"Once you set them, everyone will respect them."
Truth: They require consistent reinforcement (and that's okay!)

Daily Affirmation:

"My boundaries express self-love, not selfishness."

B.R.A.V.E ACTION STEPS

1. Identify one boundary myth you've believed.
2. Write down how it's held you back.
3. Create a new, empowering truth.
4. Share your insight in our community.

Remember: Progress over perfection. Your boundaries don't have to be perfect to be effective!

YOUR BOUNDARY TRUTH CHECKLIST

✓ They protect, not punish
✓ They connect, not control
✓ They evolve, not restrict
✓ They respect, not reject

PARTING THOUGHTS

Understanding what boundaries really are (and aren't) is your first step to freedom. They're not about building walls - they're about creating space for joy, peace, and authentic connections.

Ready to embrace the truth about boundaries? Start by letting go of one myth today. Your future self will thank you!

12. The BRAVE Action Plan

BECAUSE 'WINGING IT' ISN'T ACTUALLY A STRATEGY

A goal without a plan is just a wish... and wishes don't set boundaries!

— UNKNOWN

During a recent Blissful Besties call, I shared how my first attempt at boundaries looked like throwing spaghetti at a wall—messy and not very effective. What I needed (and what you and I deserve) was a clear roadmap. So, let's create your personalized boundary action plan!

STEP 1: YOUR BOUNDARY REALITY CHECK

Your Boundary Reality Check

Take a moment to rate yourself on these areas:

1 = "What boundaries?"
5 = "Boundary Queen")

- ☐ Work/Life Balance
- ☐ Family Dynamics
- ☐ Friend Circles
- ☐ Digital Space
- ☐ Personal Time
- ☐ Energy Management

Pro Tip: There are no wrong answers here! Remember our mantra: Progress over perfection.

THE B.R.A.V.E BLUEPRINT

B - Begin Where You Are

Choose your starting point:

- Seeking Balance: Just discovering boundaries
- Ready for Growth: Setting some boundaries, but needs consistency
- Momentum Builder: Ready to level up existing boundaries

One of my Empowered & Aligned clients started "Seeking Balance." Her first tiny step? A 10-minute morning coffee ritual without her phone. Three months later, she's confidently setting boundaries in board meetings!

R - Recognize & Respond

Create your personal boundary toolkit:

- Identify your top 3 boundary breakers
- List your common people-pleasing triggers
- Draft your go-to responses
- Plan your self-care backup strategies

A - Action Steps Timeline

Week 1-2: Foundation Phase

- Choose ONE small boundary
- Practice your response scripts
- Document resistance and wins

Week 3-4: Building Phase

- Add a second boundary
- Refine your responses
- Celebrate small victories

Week 5-6: Strengthening Phase

- Layer in digital boundaries
- Add work/life boundaries
- Track your energy levels

V - Validate & Value

Track Your Progress:

- Energy level changes
- Relationship improvements
- Stress reduction
- Joy increases
- Time reclaimed

E - Evolve & Expand

Next Level Growth:

- Advanced boundary setting
- Teaching others
- Creating lasting change

Your 90-Day Success Metrics:

✓ Morning routine established
✓ Work hours protected
✓ Digital boundaries set
✓ Family time sacred
✓ Self-care non-negotiable

IMPLEMENTATION TOOLS

The Boundary Tracker

Daily Check-In Questions:

1. Did I honor my boundaries today?
2. Where did I feel strongest?
3. What needs tweaking?
4. What wins can I celebrate?

The Response Library

Keep these handy:

- "I'll check my calendar and get back to you."
- "That doesn't work for me."
- "I need time to consider that."
- "I'm not available for that."

The Support Squad System

Join our Blissful Besties community where you can:

Share wins and challenges
Celebrate progress
Get real-time support

Daily Affirmation:

"My boundaries reflect my self-worth, and both are growing stronger every day."

B.R.A.V.E ACTION STEPS

1. Choose your starting point
2. Pick ONE boundary to begin
3. Draft your response scripts
4. Set up your tracking system
5. Plan your celebration milestones

Remember: You don't have to transform everything overnight. Start with one tiny boundary, celebrate every win, and watch the momentum build!

Your Permission Slip:

- You have permission to start small.
- You have permission to be imperfect.
- You have permission to adjust as needed.
- You have permission to celebrate progress.

PARTING THOUGHTS

This isn't about becoming a boundary perfectionist - it's about creating a life where you feel respected, energized, and authentically you. Your B.R.A.V.E journey starts with one small step.

Ready to begin? Choose your starting point and let's make those boundaries work for you!

13. What to Say When

YOUR POCKET GUIDE TO BOUNDARY SCRIPTS
THAT ACTUALLY WORK

Having the right words can make the difference between a boundary and a breakdown.

— UNKNOWN

During one of my book studies, we had an amazing breakthrough moment. As we discussed emotional reactions, one of our members blurted out, "I just wish I had a cheat sheet of exactly what to say!" Well, my boundary-setting friend, your wish is my command.

THE B.R.A.V.E WAY TO SAY WHAT YOU MEAN

B - Basic Scripts for Everyday Boundaries

For Family:

- "I love you AND I need some alone time."
- "I can visit for two hours on Sunday."
- "Let's plan for holiday hosting this year."

Beth used to dread family dinners because they turned into impromptu therapy sessions. Her game-changing script? "I hear you're going through a lot. I'm not qualified to give advice, but I can recommend some great resources." Simple, compassionate, and clear!

R - Response Scripts for Common Pushback

When They Say: "But you always help!"
You Say: "I've helped before, and now I'm setting a new boundary."

When They Say: "I thought we were friends..."
You Say: "We are friends, AND I need to honor my limits."

When They Say: "Just this once?"
You Say: "Not this time, but I appreciate your understanding."

A - Assertive Scripts for Work

For Colleagues:

- "I'm focusing on deadlines until 2 PM. Let's connect after."
- "I don't check email after 6 PM. I'll respond tomorrow."
- "My calendar is blocked for focused work time."

For Clients:

- "My business hours are 9-5 Central Time."
- "Here's when I'm available for our next session..."
- "Let's schedule this for regular business hours."

V - Virtual World Boundaries

For Social Media:

- "I take social media breaks on weekends."
- "I'll respond to DMs during office hours."
- "Thanks for thinking of me! I'm not taking on new commitments right now."

For Text Messages:

- "Got your text! I'm unplugged after 7 PM. Talk tomorrow?"
- "Thanks for reaching out! Let's schedule a proper catch-up."
- "Love you! In family time now - I'll call tomorrow."

E - Emergency Response Scripts

When People "Need" You Right Now:

- "I hear this is urgent for you. I can help tomorrow at 10 AM."
- "This sounds important. Let's discuss during regular hours."
- "I understand you're stressed. Here are some immediate resources..."

SITUATION-SPECIFIC SCRIPTS

The Holiday Helper Scripts

- "We're doing our own thing this year."
- "We can visit for [specific time] on [specific day]."
- "Let's take turns hosting - what works for you?"

The Money Boundary Scripts

- "That's not in my budget right now."
- "I don't mix friendship and finances."
- "I'm not in a position to lend money."

The Time Protector Scripts

- "I need to check my calendar first."
- "Let me get back to you tomorrow."
- "I'm booked until [specific date]."

The Energy Guardian Scripts

- "I need to recharge today."
- "I'm taking some quiet time."
- "Not today, but let's plan for next week."

Script Customization Workshop:

Fill in the blanks to create your own:
"I appreciate _____, AND I need _____."
"I can _____ instead of _____."
"Let's find a way to _____ that works for both of us."

Remember: Delivery Matters!

- Stay calm
- Keep it simple
- Don't over-explain
- Be consistent

Your Emergency Script Kit:

Keep these on your phone for quick access:

- "I need to think about that."
- "That doesn't work for me."
- "I'll get back to you tomorrow."

Daily Affirmation:

"I have the right words at the right time to protect my peace."

B.R.A.V.E ACTION STEPS

1. Choose three go-to scripts.
2. Practice them in the mirror.
3. Use them this week.
4. Share your success in our community.

Pro Tips:

- Add emojis for text responses—make it fun.
- Save templates in your phone.
- Practice with a friend or using a mirror.
- Celebrate using them!

PARTING THOUGHTS

Having scripts ready isn't about being rigid - it's about being prepared. Think of them as your boundary emergency kit. You might not need them all, but isn't it nice to know they're there?

Ready to use your new scripts? Start with one this week. Remember, even Wonder Woman had to practice with her lasso!

14. Progress Over Perfection

YOUR 90-DAY JOURNEY FROM 'EEK!' TO 'I'VE GOT THIS!'

Rome wasn't built in a day, and your boundaries won't be either (thank goodness, because who has that kind of time)?

— UNKNOWN

During a recent session, we talked about emotional reactions and how they can derail our best intentions. One member confessed, "I keep waiting for the perfect moment to start setting boundaries!" Here's the truth: There is no perfect moment, only perfect intentions.

YOUR B.R.A.V.E 90-DAY JOURNEY

Week 1-4: The Foundation Phase (AKA "Baby Steps")

B - Begin Where You Are

Week 1:

- Choose ONE tiny boundary
- Practice your scripts
- Document your feelings
- Celebrate EVERY win

One of my Empowered & Aligned clients (let's call her Jessica) started with just one boundary: no phone during her morning coffee. "It felt so small," she laughed, "but that 15 minutes of peace changed everything!"

Week 2-4:

- Add one small boundary per week
- Track your energy levels
- Notice what works
- Adjust as needed

Common Week 1-4 Pitfalls:

- Trying too much too soon
- Forgetting to celebrate small wins
- Expecting perfection
- Giving up after one "no"

Week 5-8: The Growth Phase (AKA "Finding Your Groove")

R - Recognize & Reinforce

Week 5-6:

- Add work boundaries
- Practice digital limits
- Build your support system
- Document your progress

A - Authentic Action

Week 7-8:

- Layer in family boundaries
- Strengthen friend boundaries
- Create holiday plans
- Prepare for pushback

Common Week 5-8 Challenges:

- Guilt creeping back in
- Old habits sneaking up
- Others testing limits
- Forgetting your why

Week 9-12: The Mastery Phase (AKA "Making It Stick")

V - Validate & Value

Week 9-10:

- Notice energy shifts
- Celebrate improvements
- Share your wins
- Support others

E - Empower & Evolve

Week 11-12:

- Fine-tune your system
- Plan next steps
- Build on success
- Create lasting change

YOUR WEEKLY CHECK-IN GUIDE:

Monday: Set your intention

- What's your focus boundary?
- Where might you need support?
- What's your self-care plan?

Wednesday: Mid-week reality check

- What's working?
- What needs tweaking?
- Where do you need help?

Friday: Celebration time!

- What wins can you celebrate?
- What lessons did you learn?
- How will you reward yourself?

Progress Markers (Not Perfection Demands):

Month 1:

✓ One solid morning boundary
✓ Basic scripts ready
✓ Support system in place

Month 2:

✓ Work boundaries growing
✓ Digital limits working
✓ Confidence building

Month 3:

✓ Family boundaries strong
✓ Friend circles adjusted
✓ New normal emerging

COMMON STUMBLING BLOCKS (AND HOW TO ROCK THEM)

The Guilt Trip

1. Notice it: Catch those guilt-inducing thoughts --"But they need me!" (and/or) "What will they think?"
2. Name it: Call it what it is - learned people-pleasing, not actual responsibility.
3. Navigate through it:

Use your B.R.A.V.E tools:

1. Take a deep breath
2. Remember your worth
3. Ask yourself: "Would I want my best friend feeling guilty about this?"
4. Choose peace over people-pleasing
5. Celebrate choosing yourself

The Backslide

It's normal: Even boundary pros have wobbly moments. Your old "yes" habits took years to build. New patterns take time to stick. Every step forward counts, even after two steps back

It's temporary: Think of it like boundary training wheels. Each "oops" teaches you something. Your boundary muscles get stronger with every reset. Tomorrow is always a fresh start.

It's fixable: Your comeback plan:

- Return to your smallest, easiest boundary
- Remind yourself why you started
- Reach out to your support squad
- Reset without the shame spiral

The Pushback

Expected: Consider it proof you're growing

- People don't push against doormat
- Resistance means your boundaries are working
- Their discomfort isn't your responsibility

Educational: Every pushback teaches you

- What triggers you need extra support for
- Which scripts work best
- How strong you really are

Evolutionary: Watch the transformation

- People adjust to your new normal
- Relationships either grow or go
- Your confidence builds with each boundary victory

Your Permission Slips:

Permission to start small

- One tiny boundary is better than no boundary
- Baby steps still move you forward
- Small wins create big momentum
- Your pace is the right pace.

Permission to mess up

- Perfect boundaries don't exist.
- Learning curves are normal.
- Every "mistake" is actually data.
- You're not failing, you're learning.

Permission to try again

- Today's a new day.
- Yesterday doesn't determine your worth.
- Each reset strengthens your power.
- You're building a new normal.

Permission to celebrate progress

- Every small win counts.
- Notice your growth.
- Share your victories.
- Be proud of your journey.

Kate kept a "Permission Journal." Every time she felt guilty about a boundary, she'd write herself a new permission slip. My favorite was: 'I give myself permission to leave the group chat that drains my energy.' Small? Maybe. Life-changing? Absolutely!

Remember: You're not just setting boundaries - you're creating a whole new way of living. And yes, you have permission to do it imperfectly!

Daily Affirmation:

"I'm building my boundary muscles one tiny flex at a time."

B.R.A.V.E ACTION STEPS

1. Choose your starting boundary.
2. Set up your tracking system.
3. Plan your celebrations.
4. Join our community support.

Remember: You're not behind, you're exactly where you need to be!

PARTING THOUGHTS

This journey isn't about becoming perfect at boundaries - it's about becoming perfectly comfortable with progress. Every tiny step forward is a win, every setback is a lesson, and every day is a new chance to grow.

Ready to start your 90-day journey? Remember: The only wrong way to do this is to not start at all!

15. Conclusion

YOUR PERMISSION SLIP TO PUT YOURSELF FIRST

You've made it! Whether you devoured this book in one sitting (hello, fellow achiever!) or took it chapter by chapter, you're here. And that means you're ready to transform your "yes" into a life lived on your own terms.

Throughout this journey, we've explored:

- Why boundaries aren't just nice-to-have but necessary. (Chapter 1)
- The different types of boundaries you can set. (Chapter 2)
- How to say "sorry, not sorry" with grace. (Chapter 3)
- Practical techniques that actually work. (Chapter 4)
- The amazing benefits waiting for you. (Chapter 5)
- How to handle the inevitable pushback. (Chapter 6)
- The long-term magic of maintaining boundaries. (Chapter 7)
- Common myths that might have held you back. (Chapter 8)

- Your B.R.A.V.E action plan for success. (Chapter 9)
- Ready-to-use scripts for every situation. (Chapter 10)
- A 90-day roadmap to make it all happen. (Chapter 11)

"When I started Thankful Hearts Coaching, I made a promise to myself and my clients: we would focus on progress over perfection. Every day, I witness incredible women like you taking brave steps toward living life on their own terms. It starts with one small boundary, one tiny 'no,' one moment of choosing yourself."

Remember: This isn't about becoming a boundary perfectionist. It's about creating space for joy, peace, and authenticity in your busy life. It's about finally putting yourself first without the guilt trip attached.

YOUR NEXT B.R.A.V.E STEPS

B - Begin Where You Are

- Choose one small boundary to start
- Trust that you're ready
- Know that imperfect action beats perfect inaction

R - Recognize Your Growth

- Celebrate every tiny win
- Document your progress
- Share your success with others

A - Act with Authenticity

- Use your new scripts
- Stand firm in your worth
- Trust your intuition

V - Value Your Journey

- Each step matters
- Every "no" builds strength
- Your peace is priceless

E - Evolve at Your Pace

- Progress over perfection
- Small steps, big impact
- Consistent growth wins

Your Permission Slip:

I, [Your Name], hereby give myself permission to:

- Put myself first without guilt
- Say no without explanation
- Live life on my own terms
- Choose peace over people-pleasing
- Celebrate my progress, not perfection

One of my Blissful Besties recently shared something powerful: "I used to think boundary-setting was selfish. Now I realize it's self-preservation. My only regret? Not starting sooner."

Remember: Your "yes" needs a best friend called "no" not because you're mean, not because you're selfish, but because YOU'RE worth protecting. Your time, your energy, your peace - they're all precious resources that deserve to be honored.

Ready to start your boundary journey? Remember, you don't have to do it alone. Join our Blissful Besties community where we celebrate every win, support every step, and remind each other that progress beats perfection every single time.

Your future self is thanking you for picking up this book. Now, let's make her proud by taking that first brave step toward a life lived on your own terms.

Because you deserve to live life on your own terms.

Because your peace matters.

Because it's finally your turn.

Welcome to your boundary revolution!

Thank You

FOR SAYING YES TO YOURSELF

Thank You for Saying Yes to Yourself

You didn't just read a book — you made a bold decision to choose yourself, honor your truth, and step into a life aligned with your worth. That takes courage, compassion, and commitment.

Whether this is your first brave boundary or your fiftieth, I want you to know: I see you. I celebrate you. And I'm cheering wildly for your continued growth.

If this book helped you in any way — if a chapter sparked a shift, or a sentence made you feel seen — I'd love to hear from you.

Come find me on Instagram @the.jennifer.anderson or leave a review to help another woman say yes to herself too.

You're not alone on this journey — we're in this together.

With deep gratitude,
Jen

Let's Keep the Momentum Going

You've done the inner work. You've started setting boundaries that reflect your worth. Now let's keep that progress going — together.

Whether you're craving community, personalized support, or structured accountability, I've created programs that meet you right where you are:

BLISSFUL BESTIES

A monthly membership for women ready to stop overthinking, start showing up, and surround themselves with positive, supportive energy.

Inside Blissful Besties, you'll:

- Tackle on specific mindset topic each month
- Celebrate small wins without guilt
- Join weekly live calls where you get instant coaching on that month's topic

- Get encouragement, clarity, and confidence

It's your safe space to be seen, supported, and inspired.

EMPOWERED & ALIGNED

My premium 1:1 coaching experience for high-achieving women ready to stop settling and start living fully.

Inside Empowered & Aligned, we:

- Identify and shift limiting beliefs
- Build custom boundaries that honor your truth
- Create an actionable roadmap toward a life that feels authentically yours

This is deep, personal transformation — with real accountability and tailored guidance every step of the way.

MOMENTUM MAKERS

A small-group progress partnership where consistency is the goal and perfection isn't required.

Momentum Makers includes:

- Weekly group coaching sessions
- Ongoing support, check-ins, and action plans
- Tools for tracking your habits, energy, and focus

It's the perfect space if you've got big dreams and just need the structure (and support) to get there.

READY TO TAKE THE NEXT STEP?

Book your free Pathfinder Session to discover which program fits your needs best:

https://tidycal.com/coachjen48/ pathfinder-session-discover-your-coaching-needs

You're not meant to do this alone. Let's keep building a boundary-powered life — together.

Acknowledgments

It takes a village to bring a message to life — and this book would not exist without mine.

To **Leesa Mannon**,

Thank you for your expert editing, thoughtful feedback, and the care you poured into every chapter. Your ability to polish my words while preserving my voice is a true gift, and I'm so grateful for your partnership on this journey.

To **Tara Hayes** and **Tarafied Publishing Co**,

Thank you for helping me bring this book to life in such a powerful and beautiful way. Your expertise, encouragement, and eye for detail made this process smoother than I could have ever imagined. I am deeply thankful for your support and guidance every step of the way.

To the early readers and clients who saw pieces of themselves in these pages,

Thank you for reading with open hearts, offering your reflections, and sharing your beautiful testimonials. Your words not only encouraged me during the writing process but will also guide other women to the transformation they've been searching for. Your bravery, honesty, and support mean more than you know.

And above all, to the One who planted this purpose in my soul

Thank you for turning my pain into purpose and my calling into a catalyst for change.

About the Author

Best-selling author Jen Anderson is the founder of Thankful Hearts Coaching and creator of the B.R.A.V.E method. Featured on NBC, CBS, ABC, and FOX, she helps busy women stop saying "yes" to everything so they can finally put themselves first and live life on their own terms. As a certified Life Coach, Health Coach, Transformation Coach, and Mastery Transformation Coach, she brings both expertise and real-world experience to her signature "Beliefs + Boundaries = Bliss" approach.

After her own journey from people-pleasing to peace-finding (and an eye-opening moment with Rachel Hollis' "Girl, Wash Your Face"), Jen transformed her natural ability to advise friends into a thriving coaching practice. Now, through her popular programs like Empowered & Aligned and Blissful Besties, she guides women who are ready to break free from the exhausting cycle of people-pleasing. She shows them that true bliss is possible and theirs for the taking.

When she's not helping clients discover the joy of saying "no," you can find Jen in Nebraska, probably planning her next trip, because her true bliss is traveling. Her approach to boundaries, like her coaching style, focuses on progress over perfection, sprinkled with humor and grounded in real-life application.

Connect with Jen:

Website: www.thankfulheartscoaching.com

www.ingramcontent.com/pod-product-compliance
Lightning Source LLC
Chambersburg PA
CBHW070339130626
46556CB00007B/2940